WOW – WHAT

I am so not going to make this book long. I truly do not want or need to make it long. Therefore, I am going to add fillers if I can.

It's May 25, 2021, and I cannot make heads of tails of my life or anything this morning thus, I feel sick; as if I am going to throw up. My stomach is in an uproar cold wise, and the flame; mucus is a lot; plenty.

No, it's not Covid-19 I am getting. The weather has been hot as of late and yesterday was a bit nippy for me. I had to wear my shawl to walk my dog and I do sleep with my window open. Now, I am getting a bit sick, but this is truly normal for me. My body is so not like yours. I should be fine once I have a coffee but right now, I am so not up to walking my dog. I've been up since after 7 and it's not 8 o'clock as yet.

Yes, I slept good despite the fireworks that was happening. Went to bed late and after 12am say almost 12:30, my son gave me a bit of chicken and fries. Ate a little and shared a couple pieces with my dog before going to sleep. Slept good then had to wake up to go to the bathroom. I cannot tell you the time but going back to bed I closed my eyes, and this is what I saw.

Certain things I know when I close my eyes and see things. Meaning, when I close my eyes and see the faces of people, I know death is coming to people. Sometimes the faces turn gruesome therefore, some and or, the people I see are going to die a gruesome death. Other than that, I do not put any merit to my visions because I cannot pinpoint them, nor know what they mean.

These visions I have to put merit to because wow and what; my shock factor if it is appropriate. What I see vision wise, and dream wise I cannot get away from.

What I feel spirit wise I cannot get away from.

What I know I cannot get away from, nor do I want or need to get away from what I know.

God, I cannot get away from despite me feeling the relationship I have with God is severed due to my decision of not planting a seed, or plant in the land I am living in. Yes, God is disappointed in me, but it's the reality I have to live with until I see God face to face.

Yes, God is hurt but; I cannot help it. I cannot plant in a land I do not truly love, or love. This is my reality, but God cannot and will not comprehend this; my goodness and truth. Planting good and clean is important to me.

Planting is important to God.

How you plant is truly important thus, many plant faulty; unclean, and I cannot do that to God and Mother Earth. It is truly not fair or just to me and them. And yes, God will show me otherwise if I am wrong.

Now, these visions I could not let go of. Thus, my visions spilling over into my dream world in a different way. Someone or something do not want or need me to forget therefore, I am letting you know in this book.

Saw as clear as day this plane; _Jumbo Jet_ on water. _You could not see the tail end of the plane._ All you could see was the front towards the back without the tail end of the plane on water. The plane looked submerged. The tail end was still under water. There were no survivors on the plane. In the vision all had perished, *and you could feel the eerie feeling of death.* I did not see any dead bodies. I only felt the eerie feeling of death. Allelujah. It was as if they; someone had lifted the plane out of the water. There were no debris just the plane nor could you see anyone lifting the plane. And though it was a Jumbo Jet, *you also got the feeling of old.* Like this was from the past.

So, with that said, I do not know if planes are going to crash. No, I should not say that because, I did warn the Aviation Industry of what I saw in the book proceeding this one. *WHAT ABOUT US.* Therefore, it is imperative for them; the Aviation Industry to ensure they check any planes that is going up in the air not matter the designation of the plane. It could be a helicopter or a rocket, ensure you check your planes and or, flying apparatuses thoroughly before sending them up. I do not care if it's someone who flies personally for self, check your planes and or, flying apparatus.

Further, I do not know if they are going to be excavating old planes in the South Pacific because I got the feeling of this. So yes, someplace somewhere, a plane is going to get excavated if that is the proper wording. And I am going to leave this alone because Earth is changing, and I cannot fully pinpoint my visions.

My other vision had to do with water and trees. The water was murky and or, cloudy but I could see trees this specific tree at the bottom of the water. I did not count the trees, but I remember one distinct one. So, I do not know if a land no, not a land _but_ _specifically Australia and or, a land in the South Pacific_ _is going to sink literally._

In the vision, I thought it weird for lack of a better word. Thus, I wondered if God was making lands under the sea rise up. So, I do not know if a land is going to come up out of the sea. But I gather, Australia and or, the South Pacific something is going on there.

I did not see lava just cloudy and murky water and the trees and or, tree in the water. So, I do not know if there is activity going on in Australia and the South Pacific that is not being detected by humans. _The Marianas Trench_ _and or, what Faultline is rumbling right now, but from_ _Guam to Australia; all of the South Pacific something is_ _truly not right._ _And I am going to leave things as is. Visions are things I cannot pinpoint therefore, I truly leave them alone._

After seeing those visions, was I connecting to a higher source; energy?

Yes

I was calling out to Lovey and eventually went back to sleep then my dream world took over.

I dreamt this stage; entertainment area as you would see at a concert or award show. I cannot remember the full extent of the dream, but the dream had to do with this young black female in her late teens and or, early twenties. She was being introduced and she smiled at me. She was happy. Then Terrence J. the American Actor came into the picture. He was dressed in full black. Black t-shirt and black pants. He came up to me and I said, it's been a long time. He smiled, hugged me as if he was all over me and or, on top of me, and I think he kissed me, but I am not 100% sure of the kiss.

He said, something about calling him and I told him, **_"how can I call you when I don't have a number for you"_**, and he gave me his number. I said, something to him about him giving me his number **_"when I don't have pen and paper."_**

So that hug was not good hence my sickness this morning that I am now over as of 8:25am. My tummy is not in an uproar. It has settled down and the mucus flare up is no longer there. My sickness at times is not your normal sickness. I had to write before I took my dog out hence, my tiredness and not wanting to take her out so early this morning.

Black is death for me. I truly loathe seeing anyone in Black. So yes, evil want to devour me. Therefore, not all in the Black Community is clean.

Many will side with Death to devour me. Thus, I see the crap of shit they do before it happens. I now have to be careful how I walk, and who I speak/talk to. And no, I will not worry about Evil Blacks. I know their end already.

So yes, this dream is for me. There is someone dark – black not in colour of skin, but death that is back although he's a Black Man.

I cannot take his bait despite him still trying to and wanting to get to know me relationship wise. Yes, he's from the Caribbean, but darkness surrounds him, and walk with him. He is true death, and you will not comprehend this.

Yes, to all I need, I will get from him, but material possessions mean absolutely nothing to me. I cannot dirty myself with dirty people. Therefore, he's not the right one for me. <u>I have sight to see therefore, I have to protect my life.</u>

It is still a bit cool because I felt the cool breeze touching my skin just now.

So, after that happened with me and Terrence J. I was now with a beautiful black baby. I was holding the baby in my hand and the young black girl wanted to hold the baby. So, I brought the baby to her, and she held the baby in her hands. She was on stage now. After that, I took the baby. And no, I was not the mother of the child someone else was. But wow, the baby was gorgeous.

I truly do not know what baby signifies in my dream world if they signify change, growth, happiness, death or what. So, that part of the dream I am so going to leave alone.

Now after that, still at the event but not the same as the one I was at with the Young Black Girl, the Baby, and Terrence J.

This time it was with Katy Perry, and Kelly Clarkson. Kelly Clarkson was not as chubby, and she had shaved the sides of her head.

Her hair was green. I am pretty sure it was green. She was saying something about her entrance. She had had a grand entrance with her being high up in the air on a rope and descending on stage with flares going. So, she went up high to show me the entrance. Now, Katy Perry was below. This Black Guy, random Black Guy began to sing, and he motioned her to sing with him. In the dream it was a Rihanna song he was singing but the song he was singing was **TENDER by Patrice Roberts.** Katy could not remember the lyrics to the song therefore, she could not sing the song. In the end, the Black Guy tried to kiss her, but she did not allow him to, and he went off hurriedly as if running away from her.

I will not analyze this part of the dream because I truly do not care for the American Music and or, Entertainment Industry.

I truly do not care about American Musical Artists, talk show hosts or if the industry rebound sale wise musically, or concert wise, or show wise. Things are changing and if we as people including Black People truly do not wisen up and see what is happening around us, we will never wake up from the deadly sleep we are in.

I do not know when Mother Earth is going to connect with me again, but hopefully soon.

Right now, my feel is not of hope for the human race. ***It's one of dread.*** It's like this eerie feeling is outside and I can see it, feel it. Yes, the sun is shining, and the birds are chirping, but I cannot see hope or feel hope. I know you will not be able to comprehend this, but this is it. Something is truly not right and the governments including you the people of the world are not seeing this. You are too wrapped up in the lies they are telling you when it comes to Covid-19. Yes, ***"THE GLOBAL SLAVERY"*** that was enacted on the lots of you.

Slavery that took your Fundamental Rights and Freedom from you, and you don't even know it.

Cannot see it.

Don't want to see it, and more.

You are too wrapped up in their Vaccines of Death.

People are being manipulated.
You are being controlled.
You cannot buy what you want to buy.

You cannot go out there and eat what you want to eat.

You cannot travel the way you want to travel.

You cannot bury your family when you need to bury them.

You cannot go out until when they tell you to go out.

You cannot get medical care the way you want and need to.

Take a good look at the Cemeteries of Death.

I live right where there is a Funeral Home. Trust me, you would figure with all the death's due to Covid -19 the Funeral Home next to me would be hella busy, but it isn't.

God and Death isn't stupid, it is humans that are stupid. We put people in power that scam us, lie to us, take our fundamental humans from us, and you go along with them.

Aye yes, their *"REVELATIONS"* of Death's Book. Man's so-called Holy Bible.

Now, let me ask you this. WHO PUT THEM; YOUR LEADERS, AND PHARMACEUTICAL GIANTS IN POWER?

Now tell me. WHY ARE YOU ALLOWING JACKASSES TO TAKE YOUR HUMAN RIGHTS FROM YOU?

WHY ARE YOU ALLOWING PHARMACEUTICAL COMPANIES; MONSTERS TO TAKE YOUR FUNDAMENTAL HUMANS RIGHTS FROM YOU?

WHY ARE YOU ALLOWING THESE PHARMACEUTICAL COMPANIES TO TAKE YOUR LIFE; KILL YOU?

*THEY ARE NOT GOD. SO, **WHY ARE YOU ALLOWING DEMONS TO TAKE YOUR LIFE?***

*NO, TRULY; **WHY ARE YOU ALLOWING DEMONS TO LITERALLY CONTROL YOU?***

Now tell me. HOW DID THESE VIRUSES AND DISEASES COME ABOUT?

HAVE YOU LOOKED AT THE LABS OF MEN?

Humans are truly wicked unto humans thus, **HUMANS TRULY DO NOT THINK OF THE HELL THEY ARE GOING TO FACE ONCE THEIR SPIRIT SHED THE FLESH.**

If you as a human think this is it; once you die that's it, you had truly better think again because; **THERE IS A SPIRITUAL LIFE AND A SPIRITUL DEATH.**

I will tell you again in this book.

"THE LIFE YOU LIVE HERE ON EARTH DETERMINE(S) WHERE YOU GO ONCE THE SPIRIT SHED THE FLESH."

So, if you have racked up unthinkable amounts of sins here on Earth, truly woe be unto you because; **EVERY SIN COME WITH A PRICE – DEATH PENALTY.**

I've told you in other books, the cost of 1 Sin is 1 152 000 000 years in hell and this cost does not include the days, months, years, leap years you have done that 1 Sin for.

I've also told you, Hell's Time is not like Physical Time. 24 000 years equal 1 day. Therefore, time is reversed in hell. So, your spirit have to spend 24 000 Earth Years in Hell for 1 day to be knocked off and or, taken off your Sin Record. Now imagine the rest of your sins that have and has not been tabulated yet.

Hell hath no water.
Hell hath no air conditioners.
Hell hath no fans.
Hell hath no food.
Hell is barren.

Yes, made up of a special fire that burn your spirit.

There are no Cooling Systems in Hell. So, how are you going to live; make it?

Earth did not have to be this way. We as humans made Earth this way.

We believe in lies.
Tell lies on everything.
Tell lies on God.
Tell lies on Space.
Tell lies on the Moon.

Now tell me, with all the lies we tell and believe in, how are you to live, or have life once the Spirit shed the Flesh?

And please don't tell me Jesus died to save all.

"JESUS CANNOT DIE TO SAVE ALL."

"GOD WOULD NEVER EVER PERMIT A CHILD OF LIFE – THE SAVED TO SAVE THE UNCLEAN; DEATH'S WICKED AND EVIL OWN."

"GOD WOULD NEVER EVER SACRIFICE A CHILD OF LIFE TO DEATH BECAUSE GOD IS NOT DEATH, AND GOD KNOWS NOT DEATH."

"GOD DID NOT CREATE DEATH. WE AS HUMANS CREATED OUR OWN DEATH WITH OUR SINS."

"WE AS HUMANS ARE THE ONE TO GIVE RISE AND BIRTH TO DEATH."

"ABSOLUTELY NO ONE CAN DIE TO SAVE YOU. THAT PERSON HAVE TO;

MUST LIVE; BE OF LIFE TO SAVE YOU COME ON NOW."

"WE ARE NOT ALL GOD'S CHILDREN AND PEOPLE THEREFORE, GOD CANNOT SAVE ALL."

We as humans are so wrapped up in the Bible of Men that not one of you know that the **BIBLE OF MEN; MAN HAVE AND HAS DECEIVED YOU.** Yes, took you; your life from you and from God.

Look into the Bible and see how nasty man has and have made God.

Look into the Bible and see how inept man has and have made God.

Look into the Bible and see how man has and have made God a giver backer taker, and LAW BREAKER.

Look into the Bible and see how man has and have made God a thief, murderer, incest loving god, warmonger, strife maker, and more.

Now tell me, how can God save you when you believe in all that is nasty when it comes to God and Life?

No, come on now. God is not humanities bitch, but humans make God out to be their bitch.

So now tell me, why should God have compassion for man when; MAN – HUMANS HAVE AND HAS MADE GOD NASTY AND HEARTLESS; VILE AND UNCLEAN?

I so have to take my dog for a walk now. She's been telling me she needs to go outside her way.

And yes, if there was a way to make this book free I would. I need to start writing for free now. I don't know but my mind is telling me to start an Instagram profile, but I shy away from the limelight. I truly do not like social media in that way.

So, until later and or another day, do take care.

Michelle

It's 6:06am and I walked my dog already. Yeah me. Yesterday, I only walked her once. My right knee was acting up to the point where I could not walk at times. Just getting from my bed to the washroom was more than a chore to the pain that was in my knee.

The weather has gotten better, and this is a norm for my right knee when good weather comes. Not going to worry about it. I have a cane somewhere in my room I am just going to have keep it close by.

Plus, my right nipple has stopped burning me. I truly hate when my nipple burns to the point of annoyance. So yes, my body is truly lacking something.

Eating has become a chore for me now. Don't want to make anything to eat so my day yesterday consisted of leftovers from the night before, noodle soup, and coffee. Today, I truly do not know because I am so not hungry. I always wait until I am super hungry on some days for some reason before I find something eat. Bad on my part I know. My dream world was not that busy which was great for me. My dream world is reminding me of certain things I have but I am not going to rush things. If it happens, I am thankful and blessed.

Also, dreamt my sister was sending a barrel back home. These young kids say around 5 to 7 years of age were helping me to pack the cardboard barrel. This one particular child was crying while helping me. We were packing Jamaican Excelsior Crackers as well as, Noodles; food items in a barrel.

I know my sister is scheduled to go to Jamaica. I am hoping all goes well for her, and that she finds true happiness in all her endeavours.

My cousin is also returning home, and I wish her all the best with her and her family.

I am not going to put anything to this dream. I do not know if there is going to be food shortage in Jamaica, and I truly don't want to worry about the island. I have to let Jamaica go despite my true love for the land.

Everything I need is there except for cleanliness.

Would I hesitate to plant a seed or tree in Jamaica for God?

No, I would not hesitate *but LIKE CANADA, I CANNOT PLANT A SEED OR TREE IN JAMAICA FOR GOD.* Lovey deemed Jamaica unclean; dirty, and I have to abide by the word of God.

I cannot and will not plant a seed or tree in a dirty land for God. When you think of Sins you must know the amount of Sins Jamaica and or, Jamaicans has and have racked up for God to deem that land unclean.

So yes, you know Jamaica is Modern Day Sodom and Gomorrah therefore, GOD WILL NOT SEND ANYONE THAT IS OF LIFE IN THAT LAND. I am forbidden to go into that land despite me being born there. Therefore, know, when the Bible of Man spoke about God sending his angels into Sodom and Gomorrah; that tale; story is a more than categorical lie.

Clean; God cannot send Clean into unclean lands. This I know for a fact without doubt. So, know. God cannot send anyone clean into unclean lands.

Know this for a fact.

If God sent anyone clean into unclean lands, God would be making you unclean. Thus, causing you and God to sin. So, know the truth of God.

God cannot take the life of anyone. Therefore, God protect the good and true from sin; Death.

God cannot sin for anyone yet, the Bible of Man make God out to be a Sinner, Liar, Deceiver, and more. So now tell me.

HOW CAN GOD TRUST THE WHITE RACE WHEN THEY ARE PATHOLOGICAL LIARS?

<u>Pathological Liars that lie on God</u> and billions of you globally follow in the footsteps of these lies.

Yes, it's sad and depressing on my part that I cannot go home, but it's the way of life for me.

Yes, at times I want to break my order but; each time I want to, God remind me of Hell.

DISOBEDIENCE IS AUTOMATIC DEATH IN HELL ONCE THE SPIRIT SHED THE FLESH.

Therefore, if God gives you an order, you have to stay this order no matter how painful it is for you. Yes, bummer, but it's the way it is.

You know, I never even asked God why Jamaica?

Why deem Jamaica unclean compared to the atrocities other lands has and have done in the name of greed and death?

And no, I will not go to God and ask God that question. I know the evils of men.

I know the evils of Jamaicans, and Jamaica's past. Port Royal

I know the evils of the different lands, and Jamaica is not the only condemned; unsaved land out there.

I know God is not with many lands and people here on Earth therefore, despite God deeming Jamaica unclean; dirty; many lands globally are dirty; unclean. And yes, I can name these lands.

Yes, it's sad Jamaica is deemed unclean but as Blacks, **_we did this to ourself._**

We are the ones to dirty ourself and land.

We are the ones to not "secure our future" with God.

We were the ones to divorce God, not God divorce us.

God did not tell us to accept lies. We as Blacks accepted lies.

We were the ones to forfeit our life with God for Death.

We are the ones to commit so much sin without thinking of the consequences of each sin we engage in; do.

We are the ones to not value our land and self.

We are the ones that believe that lies is/are going to save us.

We are the ones to take self and land from God.

Oh man now I want to go back to bed and sleep. I am getting sleepy and lazy. May is almost over thank God. My room is so breezy and cool that I don't need my fan. Truly love the cool breeze because now I can go under my sheet. And, on this note, I am going to go back to bed and lay down.

Michelle

Oh God Lovey to what I just saw. I need to be your true voice and way good and true.

Lovey, you know I create stories in head in order to sleep but; **what did I just see?**

Lovey and God **this man pitch black with wings.** This is not the death that I know *but a NEW DEATH OF DARKNESS.* Lovey, I know blackness but this darkness – blackness is truly void of light.

It's after 10pm and I cannot sleep. I was just laying down and to see that darkness is truly beyond me. I truly don't know what to think. I did go back to sleep this morning as well as, slept in the afternoon. I was seeing faces before me again. I even saw me, but I turned into someone else.

My sister called me as well. She is going to take the vaccine.

Also, she is cleaning up her place, and asked me if I needed a bed, but I told her no. My bed is still fairly new. She also told me, 3 of her children took the vaccine already.

Lovey, I truly have to wonder why so many people trust the White Race with their lives?

Lovey, how can you keep, and continue to put your truth, and trust continually in a Nation and Race of People that intentionally hurt you, and kill you?

How can you keep, and continue to put your truth and trust in a Nation and Race of People that intentionally lie to you, deceive you, and more?

GOD IS LOVE Beres Hammond ft. Popcaan

Lovey, you truly need to guide and protect me for real.

Yes, I cuss out the White Race reckless and rude. Many will not like this or me.

Many Blacks will not like this, or me but I truly do not care.

Life is not about lies.
Life is not about death; killing people.

Oh God this darkness.
This man.
Who is he?
What is his purpose?
Why am I seeing him with wings?

Does his wings represent him spreading darkness; more darkness on land; well, here on Earth?

Lovey, what New Plague or Death is going to devastate Earth; humans?

In all I see Lovey. Please keep me safe and protected at all times.

Lovey, what does this all mean because I truly do not know. Oh Gad mi belly, mi belly, mi belly.

What is this I am seeing with my eyes God?

Oh God, what is this I am seeing with my eyes?

Where, how, how is this darkness possible Lovey?

Lovey, darkness could be that Black – void of life – light all together?

Oh God Lovey truly wrap your goodness and truth around me because I truly do not know.

I see but I truly do not know.

I see but I truly cannot comprehend this darkness – blackness.

I see but I truly cannot cope; grasp this darkness.

Lovey, I know our sins are ugly <u>*BUT THIS DARKNESS IS TRULY BLACKER; DARKER THAN THE SINS OF MAN,*</u> *and this I cannot comprehend.*

I cannot comprehend this great darkness – him because; I've never seen anything like this before. Especially in the form of a man with wings.

Oh God. God what do I do?

How do you cope seeing this darkness; blackness?

Please hold me because I truly do not know what to do.

Lovey and God, I cuss out the White Race; humans but humans do not comprehend the magnitude of what's out there death wise, and life wise.

Not even music can soothe be because this darkness is rattling me. Lovey, if people could see what I see; do you think they would piss their pants, and poop themselves?

Lovey, if people could see what I see, do you think they would change their dirty linen of self?

Lovey, what type of Death is this man?

Lovey, how do you stay sane seeing suck blackness?

There is absolutely no light in this darkness Lovey. Now tell me, _WHAT IS WRONG WITH HUMANS THAT THEY CANNOT SEE THEIR LIFE BEFORE THEM?_

What is wrong with humans that they do not think of their Spiritual Life and Well Being?

What is wrong with humans that they do not think of their Sins and the Cost of each Sin?

What is wrong with humans LOVEY THAT; HUMANS TRULY DO NOT WANT OR NEED LIFE, THEY HAVE TO FORFEIT THEIR LIFE TO DEATH?

Lovey, what more can I do?
How much more can I write?
How much more can I show?
How much more can I tell?
How much more can I see and tell?

How much more can I plea and beg with humans to think of their life beyond Earth?

How much more must I cuss out people and the different races for humans to wake up and see their tomorrow?

How much more must I cuss out people and the different races for humans to wake up and see their life, live their life good and true, save their goodness in you Lovey, and more?

I wanted to put fillers in this book, but I don't think I can put fillers in this book Lovey to what I am seeing when I close my eyes.

Are humans this far gone Lovey that they cannot see their death and extinction before them?

I need an escape Lovey. I truly need an escape.

Allelujah

Judgement
Judgement

HUMANITY HAS BEEN JUDGED. THUS, WOE BE UNTO MAN LITERALLY.

Oh God, my body is getting weak.

Oh God my body.
My body.
My body.

A getting weak Lovey, a getting weak.

Oh God Lovey hold me, I am weak.
But I have to carry on.
I have to come to you.
I have to ask for forgiveness.
I have to ask that you save me.
I have to rest my life and all in you.
I have to keep you good and true Lovey.
I have to keep you.

What I am seeing is truly not pretty.

Therefore, I need you to be my saving grace and righteousness day in and day out.

I need you to be my clingy vine where I can run to all the time and cling to you for safety, care, life, health, goodness and truth; all my good and true need and needs Lovey.

Lovey and God, all my wrongs done onto you truly forgive me good and true because; I truly do not know what this darkness and man represent for real.

I do not know what his wings represent either.

No, I am not scared in that way, I am just at a loss; bewildered because this darkness is something that is truly new to me.

Lovey, when we talk about darkness, this darkness I saw; is nothing compared to that darkness.

Lovey, why can't humans wake up and come back to life?

Why can't humans wake up and see what is going on around them?

Lovey, why can't humans see the darkness of self?

Lovey, why can't humans see that they are llviriy [ui Death?

It's about Life now not Death and humans truly cannot see this. Humans are so blinded that they believe anything the churches, politicians, gangs, pharmaceutical companies, and more tell them.

When do humans see their life Lovey?

When will humans see that times are changing, and it's going to get worse? Evil's time is up.

Evil must take their wicked and evil own.

Evil must die with evil Lovey come on now. Yet, this darkness bewilders me.

Truly have mercy upon me and the saved Lovey.

Truly wash me clean with your good and true waters of life.

Do not let me go down with the wicked and evil.

Truly help me to protect me and the saved here on Earth, and in the Spiritual Realm Lovey.

Truly guide and protect me so that I do not walk wrong.

Talk wrong.
Guide wrong.
Write wrong.
Sing wrong.
Sleep wrong.

Lovey, all I need is in you and right now, I truly need you.

I need you to protect and shelter me from this darkness; man.

Lovey, let me rest my head on your shoulder.

Let me find true peace and happiness with you.

Be my good and true seed and seeds Lovey.

Be my good and true plant and plants, trees, food, health, water, wealth, life source, life force, and more good and true things.

Lovey, I have to protect my life with you.
I have to make sure and ensure I am safe with you.

I have to make sure and ensure my name is in the Good Book of Life; Your Book, and Our Book good and true.

Lovey, please whatever you do, truly do not diminish my investments in you for any reason. Keep the interest growing on my investments with you because in true truth, I cannot see my life without you.

I truly do not want or need to go to hell.

At times like now, I would look out, and all I see is darkness; no light. Therefore Lovey, let our life with each other continually have good and true light. Never ever let our path and pathway be dark.

Oh God Lovey, what would I do without you.

Lovey, lifelessness is lifelessness; death.

I do not want or need anything lifeless with you come on now.

Lovey and God, what is wrong with me and you that; people are not waking up to what's happening around them?

Why are humans so carefree?

A great tribulation is coming.

Many more have to die.

Oh God
Oh God
Oh God

I need your help.
I need hope; your hope.

I need your strength Lovey. I am so weak right now, and I truly do not know what to do.

Great Death is coming and for a surety DARKNESS WILL ENGULF THE EARTH. We as humans made it so.

Lovey, many are truly not thinking about their life here on Earth right now. Many are caught up in the fame game, doing all they can to stay relevant in the limelight, but I cannot be this way. I have to come to you Lovey for my life, and the life of the good and true, and truly trying to be good. Lovey we need a safe place here on Earth with you when Judgement hit Earth full throttle.

I have to be in our safe haven Lovey.

I cannot stay in this world with the unsaved Lovey.

I have to be planting food and securing food, and clean drinking water for our good and true with you and Mother Earth Lovey.

Lovey, our harvest; the harvest of the good and true cannot be the same as the wicked and evil come on now.

I bug you so much for separation; the separation and segregation of Good and Evil. I refuse to support the wicked and evil of Earth or the Spiritual Realm, and you truly know this.

My life with you is not of evil nor do I want or need it to be. But seeing what I saw, <u>WE LOVEY AND MOTHER EARTH HAVE TO; MUST SECURE OUR GOOD AND TRUE IN THE LAND AND LANDS YOU NEED US TO BE IN.</u> This is truly important to me.

This need must be important to you as well. I need you to open up your world and realm to me Lovey. I need to know that our people will be safe here on Earth with you and Mother Earth. I need You and Mother Earth in the midst of all of this good and true

Lovey. I cannot let Death; this new death consume us and our good and true people.

Lovey, truly continue to be my good and true god and source.

Michelle
May 26, 2021

It's May 27, 2021, and God is my true hope and truth. Yes, I had a beautiful night, and my dream world was wow.

So yes, despite what I wrote in WHAT ABOUT US, and not wanting to plant a seed or tree in the land I am in. *GOD NEED ME TO PLANT HERE. I HAVE TO PLANT A SEED OR TREE OR PLANT IN THE LAND I AM IN FOR GOD.*

I cannot get around this. I HAVE TO OBEY.

God is reminding me. *GOOD FAR EXCEEDS MY LOATHING OF THIS LAND; THE HURT AND PAIN I'VE ENCOUNTERED IN THIS LAND.*

How did God remind me of this?

Family, Older White People, and Young Black Boys. It was as if I was at my sister's house, but it was not my sister's house, it was like my aunt's house. My aunt that is in the United States, but it wasn't her house either. The house was Auntie Pearl and Uncle Robbie's house. In the house there were Young Black Youths. I went to use the bathroom but could not use the bathroom in peace. Older White People males predominantly kept coming into the bathroom. Yes, I was sitting on the toilet trying to pee with these people coming in. I eventually used the bathroom in peace and washed my hand, but the water was so strong; lots of water came out of the faucet. Then, I was with my aunt from the United States. She had a wig on in the dream. Dark colour wig. She was married to Uncle Robbie, and I wondered when that happened. But it wasn't her, it was Auntie Pearl that was married to Uncle Robbie. Auntie Pearl who seemed to be my aunt was renovating her home. She put up a bed to lean up against the wall by the window I believe. The floor needed to be redone as the bed was glued to the floor. Then you saw Uncle Robbie who is White in the dream and yes, White in real life renovating and or, fixing something outside. Yes, the grass outside was green and a little piece was dry not fully dry but; as if the sun had taken the colour from that area when there isn't enough water on that spot.

My other dream had to do with planting and God showing me the beauty of this with different colours like a game for me but not like a game.

Then I dreamt my mother and she was helping me with my bins. She brought me to the garage and...no, before that I dream;

this one particular dead, the one I truly hate to see in my dreams. We were in the under ground and he was in this car. We were to go somewhere but he got stuck on the ramp of the driveway. His car could not move. So yes, I am hoping God and Death truly shut that hog – bitch down. Can't stand seeing him in my dream world.

Stay the hell in hell and burn. He's caused me too much grief in life and in his death.

Then I was with my mother. She was helping me with my bins. We took the elevator down with this White Lady and her daughter. The White Lady had a pot with a plant in it. When we got to the bottom and or, in the garage the White Lady gave her daughter the pot with the flower. Oh man, I am forgetting something. When we reached the bottom, our elevator and the other elevator opened up. This White Lady – older was waiting on the elevator and when it opened, and we got out. She kept going from one elevator to the next as if confused. Then while outside the elevator walking, the White Lady that was with me, my mother, and her daughter gave her daughter the pot with the flower. The young girl did not know what to do so we went to my garden, and she planted her flower. My garden needed work. I had planted vegetables like tomatoes, and cucumbers, and the plants were catching. Some; about 3-4 leaves where withered, and one leaf looked as if a worm had eaten some of it. Those leaves I took off to throw away.

So yes, God is reminding me of family I have in North American Lands, goodness that some Young Black Youths have and has done for me as well as, goodness that Male and Female Whites who are older has and have done for me. _So, the goodness I received from these people including family far outweighs my loathing of this land._

God is telling me. _I cannot look at my hurt and pain when it comes to this land; the land I am in._

GOD HAS ALWAYS BEEN THERE FOR ME, AND I HAVE TO DO RIGHT BY GOD. This I did forget and for this, I ask God to truly forgive me. So yes, _I HAVE TO PLANT A TREE OR SEED IN CANADA GOOD AND TRUE._

I WILL NOT TAKE THE TRUTH OF GOD FROM GOD IN THIS WAY. IT IS TRULY NOT FAIR NOR IS IT JUST TO GOD. I HAVE TO DO THE GOOD I MUST AND CAN DO FOR GOD.

I will not question God about wanting a plant or tree in Canada. God knows right from wrong better than me.

God know the heart and mind of many better than me.

God knows the future better than me. Therefore, GOD IS GOOD ALL THE TIME.

Yes, Lovey and God did not have to use family to show me things, but this is Lovey. I am glad Lovey did.

Listen, with me having to have to plant a seed in the land I am in, I don't, truly don't want America; THE UNITED STATES OF AMERICA TO BE SAVED OR BENEFIT FROM ME PLANTING THIS PLANT OR SEED.

I know, I have family in the United States but in all I do for God; it's not about my biological family in that way. I do not look at the good from my family. I just see me and God, and the goodness and truth I have for God. Yes, it's hard to explain but I cannot explain it any better.

It's just God and me in my world of goodness and truth more time.

Yes, I will forever ever plea for the saved, but I will not plea for America; the United States of America and Americans.

Selfish on my part yes, but the United States of America I truly do not want or need God to save. Dem too wicked and evil.

Death wow.

Death owns them; that land and people in my view this morning so no, I truly do not want or need to save that land despite me having family there. Black People in that land have to start thinking wise and start doing that which is right and just for self. Leave out of the Domain of Death, and respect and value your life and well being.

God has and have been trying to save Black Americans, it is Black Americans that keep ignoring God as well as, rejecting God.

"GET OUT OF BABYLON" if you can. Blacks are not safe there; In America. Oh Allelujah.

"GET OUT. GET OUT."

How much more must God warn the lots of you, _and you keep sitting in, and on the SEATS OF DEATH?_

And yes, _my loathing of the land I am in has nothing to do with hate and this is what God is reminding me of as well_.

Planting a seed or tree here is not planting in hate. I cannot plant hate, I can only plant good and true.

So yes, God is also showing me that; all the good I've received from others, has and have wiped out the pain and hurt I've felt in this land. Plus, it is in this land that I am writing good and true for God so this truly say something.

God has and have remembered Canada.

Am I disappointed that God wants a tree or a plant here in Canada?

No

It just means God still has me, and despite my true feel and truth; GOD STILL REQUIRE ME TO DO FOR GOD.

God is not giving up on me and I have to hold on to God. Therefore, A JAH WORKS – THE WORK AND BLESSINGS OF GOD.

JAH WORKS by Terror Fabulous

Despite your pain and obstacles, God is there for you no matter what.

Also, G98.7.

I do not know but somehow this radio station resonated in the dream. I do not know how it's affiliated to the dream, or if the owner was trying to reach out to me in death.

I am going to leave it alone because I truly do not know.

All I know is, _God want me to plant here, and I cannot disobey God._ I have to do what God requires of me, and I did tell you this. SO, YES, _CANADA IS ON THE DOCKET OF GOD LITERALLY, AND FOR REAL._

And I am going to end this book here because, _I DID GET MY GOOD AND TRUE ANSWER FROM GOD._

The next book, I truly do not know what the title will be. But in all you do, think of you, your life, the life of God, your future generations, and more.

God is good therefore, despite our faults and flaws, *God is there for us all.*

Michelle

BOOKS WRITTEN BY MICHELLE JEAN 2021

MY TALK JANUARY 2021

MY TALK JANUARY 2021 – BOOK TWO

MINI BOOK

JUST TALKING – THINKING

A LITTLE TALK WITH MOTHER EARTH

I NEED ANSWERS GOD

POETRY MY WAY

THE MIND AND SPIRITUALITY

I NEED ANSWERS GOD – PART TWO

MY NIGHTS

I NEED ANSWERS GOD – PART THREE

GOD IS GOOD

WHAT ABOUT US

COMING SOON

Open for now.